bright poems
for dark days

An anthology for hope

For Anne and Eldon, two lights on the horizon.

bright poems
for dark days

An anthology for hope

Julie Sutherland

Illustrated by Carolyn Gavin

FRANCES
LINCOLN

Contents

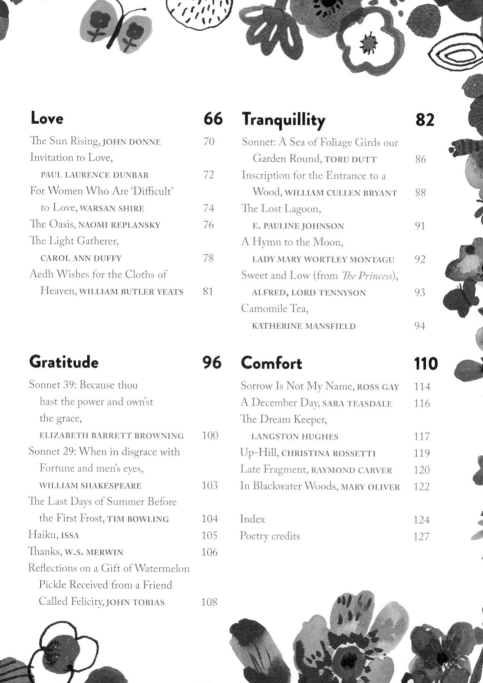

Introduction

Words have the power to heal us. This conviction has been held for thousands of years. Over the portals of the library of Pharaoh Ramses II in the thirteenth century BCE was an inscription labelling it as 'the house of healing for the soul'.[1] This engraving, recorded by an historian of Ancient Greek over two thousand years ago, fired the imaginations of Renaissance writers, who bequeathed the sentiment to centuries of accomplished poets and authors.

Today, 'reading for well-being', or 'bibliotherapy', takes place in countries around the world for diverse ends—rehabilitation in prisons, improved health in seniors with dementia, enhanced mental health for veterans, emotional resilience in cancer patients and so on. Powerful creative writing is even used to shift public attitudes towards social justice and climate change. In these ways, the purpose of reading may be vastly different from what it was when you studied poetry at school. Literature is not something to be deconstructed in order to understand its technical virtues but rather is something to be savoured for its emotional ones. It is both a window and a mirror, through which we can come to better understand others and ourselves.

This book is rooted in just such an understanding of literature's power. It doesn't recoil from the reality that life can be hard, but it resists the temptation to fixate on that point. It encourages us to try to 'see better', as the faithful Kent said to King Lear, even when the world is broken. Today, the world feels deeply damaged. Everywhere, it and we are hurting. In the last two decades alone, we have been confronted with raging wildfires. Increasing hate crimes. The depletion of non-renewable resources. The coronavirus pandemic. In these unsettling times, every flash of breaking news is enough to crack the human heart.

But though these years have brought reason to feel sorrow so too have they delivered cause for joy. Declarations on the rights of indigenous peoples have been recognised by governments and passed into law. International movements such as Fridays For Future and #MeToo have begun to hold systems and individuals to account. A nation historically steeped in slavery has seen its first Black president and its first biracial female vice president. Tyrants have fallen. Wind turbines have sprung up.

These global triumphs and tribulations often unite humankind. While some calamities fuel division, human beings endure them together. We grow determined in the face of them to find common ground and heal collectively. When we achieve great things, we also gather, on these occasions to celebrate. By contrast, personal grief, depression and anxiety separate us from the billions of humans and non-human animals with whom we share the Earth. In fact, they often alienate us from even our own families and friends.

You may have turned to this book on a day when you feel that the world is passing you by, that nobody understands you or knows your pain or has experienced your heartache, disillusionment or loss. In its pages, you just might hear your own story. This is one of poetry's most remarkable qualities: it puts into words feelings that we ourselves may have been unable to express. We read a poem and think, 'That's it! That's how I feel!'

Poets have given us language to articulate our fears, hopes, joys and sorrows. They have also laid bare their hearts. In them, we find a kindred spirit and realise we are not alone. Though we are not all the same, we share the array of emotions that bind us together into a beloved book recounting the story of humankind.

Another magnificent characteristic of poetry is its brevity. Not all poems are short, but short poems can often have the greatest impact. Percy Bysshe Shelley called poetry 'a sword of lightning, ever unsheathed, which consumes the scabbard that would contain it'. In other words, poetry is quick and forceful. Rita Dove called it 'language at its most distilled and most powerful'. Poetry is mighty, but it is also compassionate. William Wordsworth said that poetry 'is the spontaneous overflow of powerful feelings'. We as readers then wrap those feelings around us like a woolly cloak to protect us from the cold. Having short poems at the ready—perhaps ones we have committed to memory—can be a defence against a storm of negative thoughts and emotions battering to be let in.

How do you read a poem? That is entirely up to you. But we recommend that you read each one out loud, if it is possible to do so. This will help you hear and feel its rhythm, its rhyme, its musicality. It will permit you to more fully taste its sweetness or bitterness. You might also read each poem slowly so that its images more fully come to life. Let those pictures linger in your mind. Savour them. Meditate on them. Allow them into your heart and feel their warmth there. It doesn't matter if you 'get' every line of every poem. If an image, word or phrase resonates, let it dwell in your spirit without meaning or reason. Something doesn't have to make sense to be restorative.

Not all poems will speak to all people. While hundreds or even thousands of poems across the ages have sounded again and again, certain poems only ring true to a few people or at a specific time. We have chosen a variety of poems to include in this anthology for hopefulness. Many are centuries old and likely familiar. Others are newer and maybe lesser known. We trust that some of them will bring brightness to your dark days.

1* The author would like to thank Dr. Paula Byrne and Professor Sir Jonathan Bate of the ReLit Foundation for this point.

Hope

How can poetry help us to view things differently?
How can it make us less afraid?

Hope, says Emily Dickinson, is a 'thing with feathers' (p. 14). While for some readers, this sweet, light metaphor may ring true, for the more cynical among us, the image of hope as a cheerful bird who sings through every storm may not immediately resonate. In our gloomiest days, hope seems to plummet gracelessly toward the heart of darkness, not soar on weightless wings. And yet, because hope gives rise to courage, it is vital as we stumble through the dark. Hope inspires us to believe that the future is bright. As Carnevali gently reminds us in his short poem, 'Hope' (p. 16), 'Tomorrow will be beautiful'.

How can poetry help us to view things differently? How can it make us less afraid? Some poets lead by example, exploring ways to revitalise hope in vivid lyric verse. In McKay's 'I Shall Return' (p. 17), the speaker dreams of revisiting his homeland. Thoughts of beloved sapphire skies and village dances help his hope find its feathers and take flight. Reading this poem might prompt you to think about what lifts your spirits. Perhaps thoughts of love or summer kindle hope? Or witnessing a random act of kindness? Or does hope arise when you dance or play a sport? Exercise gives people a greater sense of purpose and revives positive feelings such as hope. It can also awaken gratitude and love. Perhaps you nurture hope by spending time with a friend's children or picnicking with your grandmother. Socialising helps boost our mental health: when our spirits are lifted, so too is our hope.

Most of the poems in this section are exquisitely crafted celebrations of hope. The poets weave their optimism into powerfully poetic tapestries. Just as Dickinson draws on avian imagery in her poem, so too does Sassoon employ bird imagery in 'Everyone Sang' (p. 19) to express a soldier's jubilation at the end of the First World War. The young man's soul, like a bird in flight, wings 'wildly across the white / Orchards'. After years of struggle, he is free. In this poem, music is a symbol of peace. Song is also central to Johnson's 'Lift Every Voice and Sing' (p. 20), but the music in Johnson's work crescendos before the fight for freedom has ended. Our wars might not be literal, but they feel like battles nonetheless.

Poems like Sassoon's and Johnson's that are born in darkness but focus on the light encourage us to look for flickers of dawn on our own horizons. Poetry that is not explicitly about hope can still help our flagging spirits. Their sound and sense delight us, inspire us, even uplift us. When Shelley summons a 'Spirit fierce' to be 'my spirit' in 'Ode to the West Wind' (p. 22), our own souls, caught up in the speaker's great resolve, naturally swell with bold intention.

When we step into the worlds of these poems, we are distracted from our own bleak thoughts. Our imaginations become alive as we enter into their landscapes and taste their new, sweet fruit. We catch glimpses of our future selves, alive and shimmering with great expectations. We are reminded that hope *is* a thing with feathers and that it will keep fluttering its wings. With renewed optimism, we embrace the hope that tomorrow will indeed be beautiful.

'HOPE' IS THE THING WITH FEATHERS
by EMILY DICKINSON

'Hope' is the thing with feathers —
That perches in the soul —
And sings the tune without the words —
And never stops — at all —

And sweetest — in the Gale — is heard —
And sore must be the storm —
That could abash the little Bird
That kept so many warm —

I've heard it in the chillest land —
And on the strangest Sea —
Yet — never — in Extremity,
It asked a crumb — of Me.

The bracingly original American poet Emily Dickinson (1830–1886) only posthumously achieved the recognition she deserves for her refreshing and unconventional verse. With its signature dashes, Dickinson forces the reader to slow down, take breaths and focus on individual words and phrases. The image of hope in this poem is delicate — it is a 'thing with feathers' that we soon learn is a 'little Bird' perched in each human's breast. And yet, we should not be deceived. This small being is mighty and stout-hearted. It sings without ceasing, withstands all storms, brings warmth to its bearers and never asks for anything in return.

I'VE HEARD it iN THE CHiLLEST LAND

HOPE
by EMANUEL CARNEVALI

Tomorrow will be beautiful,
For tomorrow comes out of the lake.

Emanuel Carnevali (1897–1942) was born in Florence, Italy. He immigrated to America in 1917 and swiftly gained national recognition for his gift as a poet. He suffered violent, painful illnesses throughout his short adult life, and the relentlessness of his suffering appears in much of his poetry. 'Hope' is arresting in its simplicity, yet it leaves the reader asking questions that are longer than the poem itself. What does it mean for tomorrow to come out of a lake? Is it thrust out like the mighty, magic sword Excalibur, gifted to King Arthur from the Lady of the Lake? Or does it rise up gently, like a sweet, soft mist? Perhaps the answers to these questions matter little. What matters is that 'tomorrow will be beautiful'.

I SHALL RETURN
by CLAUDE MCKAY

I shall return again; I shall return
To laugh and love and watch with wonder-eyes
At golden noon the forest fires burn,
Wafting their blue-black smoke to sapphire skies.
I shall return to loiter by the streams
That bathe the brown blades of the bending grasses,
And realize once more my thousand dreams
Of waters rushing down the mountain passes.
I shall return to hear the fiddle and fife
Of village dances, dear delicious tunes
That stir the hidden depths of native life,
Stray melodies of dim remembered runes.
I shall return, I shall return again,
To ease my mind of long, long years of pain.

Born in Jamaica in 1889, Claude McKay (d. 1948) moved to the United States as a young man, where he became a central figure in the Harlem Renaissance, a defining moment of Black cultural and intellectual history in America. In the poem here, McKay repeats the hopeful phrase 'I shall return' six times in fourteen lines. For centuries, people have chanted, prayed and engaged in other practices of repetition that quiet the mind and relax the body. Repeated phrases in poetry have a similarly tranquillising effect. 'I shall return' soothes both the speaker and the reader. The poem is nostalgic, with its alliterative phrases romanticising a period of relative ease, but it is also forward looking, to a time when the speaker will be disburdened of 'long, long years of pain'. The speaker escapes to happy memories to remind him there is reason to hope for better days ahead.

EVERYONE SANG
by SIEGFRIED SASSOON

Everyone suddenly burst out singing;
And I was filled with such delight
As prisoned birds must find in freedom,
Winging wildly across the white
Orchards and dark-green fields; on—on—and out of sight.

Everyone's voice was suddenly lifted;
And beauty came like the setting sun:
My heart was shaken with tears; and horror
Drifted away ... O, but Everyone
Was a bird; and the song was wordless; the singing will never be done.

The great English poet of the First World War, Siegfried Sassoon (1886–1967), was no stranger to suffering. The decorated soldier on the Western Front battled 'shell shock', now called PTSD (post-traumatic stress disorder), but he still wrote from time to time about exquisite moments of optimism. The imagery in 'Everyone Sang' is lush with the glory of unforeseen joy – 'everyone suddenly burst out singing'. It is rich with the hope of peace – 'the singing will never be done'. To help him express the surge of hope he feels at the end of the war, the speaker uses the simile, a figurative device which helps make an image or idea more vivid by comparing it with something else: the soldier's delight is like that of a caged bird who finds freedom. The beauty of peace is like the glorious colours of the setting sun.

LIFT EVERY VOICE AND SING
by JAMES WELDON JOHNSON

Lift every voice and sing
Till earth and heaven ring,
Ring with the harmonies of Liberty;
Let our rejoicing rise
High as the listening skies,
Let it resound loud as the rolling sea.
Sing a song full of the faith that the dark past has taught us,
Sing a song full of the hope that the present has brought us.
Facing the rising sun of our new day begun,
Let us march on till victory is won.

Stony the road we trod,
Bitter the chastening rod,
Felt in the days when hope unborn had died;
Yet with a steady beat,
Have not our weary feet
Come to the place for which our fathers sighed?
We have come over a way that with tears has been watered,
We have come, treading our path through the blood of the slaughtered,

Out from the gloomy past,
Till now we stand at last
Where the white gleam of our bright star is cast.

God of our weary years,
God of our silent tears,
Thou who hast brought us thus far on the way;
Thou who hast by Thy might
Led us into the light,
Keep us forever in the path, we pray.
Lest our feet stray from the places, our God, where we met Thee,
Lest, our hearts drunk with the wine of the world, we forget Thee;
Shadowed beneath Thy hand,
May we forever stand.
True to our God,
True to our native land.

'Lift Every Voice and Sing' by the American writer and civil rights activist James Weldon
Johnson (1871–1938) was put to music by his brother, J. Rosamond Johnson, and in 1900
it was performed by a five-hundred-voice children's choir for the late Abraham Lincoln's
birthday celebration. The first stanza is a song of rejoicing. After a darker second stanza
recounting Black people's journey from a 'gloomy past' to a shining present, the poem
finishes victoriously as they lay claim to the land they had been brought to as slaves.
The poem follows a careful rhyme scheme, but each successive stanza has an additional
line. Just as Black people refused to remain in the chains of slavery, so too does the poet
thrust the lines beyond the confines of stanzaic form.

ODE TO THE WEST WIND
by PERCY BYSSHE SHELLEY

V

Make me thy lyre, even as the forest is:
What if my leaves are falling like its own!
The tumult of thy mighty harmonies

Will take from both a deep, autumnal tone,
Sweet though in sadness. Be thou, Spirit fierce,
My spirit! Be thou me, impetuous one!

Drive my dead thoughts over the universe
Like wither'd leaves to quicken a new birth!
And, by the incantation of this verse,

Scatter, as from an unextinguish'd hearth
Ashes and sparks, my words among mankind!
Be through my lips to unawaken'd earth

The trumpet of a prophecy! O Wind,
If Winter comes, can Spring be far behind?

In his short life, Percy Bysshe Shelley (1792–1822) established himself as one of the greatest English Romantic poets. In this lyric ode, the West Wind is a powerful living spirit. Throughout the poem, the wind is connected with the cycle of seasons, and in stanza five we encounter its strength in autumn. The poet paints a picture of falling leaves, blown hither and thither by the 'tumult' of the wind's 'mighty harmonies'. Though destructive, the wind is also life-giving, and the poet asks this great force of nature to rush through him: 'Make me thy lyre'. The poem's celebration of spiritual renewal, or improved well-being, deeply resonates with many modern readers. Though autumn swiftly turns into that most ferocious of the seasons, the cycle does not end: 'If Winter comes, can Spring be far behind?'

ALL
OVERGROWN
WITH AZURE MOSS
AND FLOWERS
SO SWEET
THE SENSE
FAINTS
PICTURING
THEM!

Resilience

+

Courage

Courageous people don't have their eye on what is behind them but rather on what is ahead. This is often true of resilient people too.

The Nobel Prize-winning novelist William Faulkner emboldened readers with the line, 'You cannot swim for new horizons until you have courage to lose sight of the shore'. These words quicken our confidence because they promise new vistas. Courageous people don't have their eye on what is behind them but rather on what is ahead. This is often true of resilient people too. They are not imprisoned by disappointments, failures or regrets. In this way, courage and resilience are close relatives. A courageous human is a resilient one.

History and the present day are bursting with tales of resilient, courageous individuals. Harriet Tubman, who escaped slavery but returned to the United States on several harrowing missions to conduct hundreds of other Black people to Canada on the 'Underground Railroad'. Anne Frank, who lived in the constant awareness of being discovered by Nazis and yet whose belief in the goodness of humankind was unwavering. Helen Keller, who was attacked by an illness that left her in darkness and silence but who overcame these challenges and championed a better world for others who were visually or hearing impaired. Malala Yousafzai, who recovered from a bullet to the head and tirelessly advocates for every girl's right be educated. These are extraordinary heroes whose very names are inseparable from their acts of courage.

Other individuals whose bravery may not be so exceptional but whose resilience is remarkable can inspire us as well. These are people who get knocked down, but they get up again, as the British rock band Chumbawamba sang in their high-spirited smash hit.

Thomas Edison, who struggled at school, finally quitting, but who was vitally responsible for issuing in the modern era of electricity. James J. Braddock, the American heavyweight boxing champion who defied the odds and his weakened right hand to resurge as 'Cinderella Man'. Maya Angelou, whose childhood was marked by poverty and abuse but who became a widely respected civil rights activist and writer. Greta Thunberg, who endured bullying and confronted disordered eating before she rose to international acclaim as an indefatigable defender of the environment.

Those buoyant individuals also gained worldwide recognition. What about the unsung heroes? There are resilient human beings everywhere whose stories may never be told but whose courage is just as remarkable. The young man who asks another young man to the prom. The woman who leaves an abusive relationship. The child who stares down cancer. Can you see yourself mirrored in these brave human beings? Do they motivate you to become a more formidable version of yourself?

The poets in this section give expression to all manner of resilience and courage, from the dramatic fortitude in Henley's 'Invictus' (p. 33) to the plucky determination in Wright's 'Lines on Retirement, after Reading *Lear*' (p. 34). Resilience and courage come in myriad forms, but no matter the shape, the bearer's spirit is steadfast. To be resilient is not to be calm in the face of adversity: it is to refuse to let the adversary win. To be courageous is not to be fearless: it is to be fearful and still act. It is to swim for new horizons, resolutely refusing to look back.

STILL I RISE
by MAYA ANGELOU

You may write me down in history
With your bitter, twisted lies,
You may trod me in the very dirt
But still, like dust, I'll rise.

Does my sassiness upset you?
Why are you beset with gloom?
'Cause I walk like I've got oil wells
Pumping in my living room.

Just like moons and like suns,
With the certainty of tides,
Just like hopes springing high,
Still I'll rise.

Did you want to see me broken?
Bowed head and lowered eyes?
Shoulders falling down like teardrops,
Weakened by my soulful cries?

Does my haughtiness offend you?
Don't you take it awful hard
'Cause I laugh like I've got gold mines
Diggin' in my own backyard.

You may shoot me with your words,
You may cut me with your eyes,
You may kill me with your hatefulness,
But still, like air, I'll rise.

→

Does my sexiness upset you?
Does it come as a surprise
That I dance like I've got diamonds
At the meeting of my thighs?

Out of the huts of history's shame
I rise
Up from a past that's rooted in pain
I rise
I'm a black ocean, leaping and wide,
Welling and swelling I bear in the tide.

Leaving behind nights of terror and fear
I rise
Into a daybreak that's wondrously clear
I rise
Bringing the gifts that my ancestors gave,
I am the dream and the hope of the slave.
I rise
I rise
I rise.

Maya Angelou's (1928–2014) anthem of resilience is rooted in the American civil rights movement of which she was a vital part. With its specific references to 'the huts of history's shame', 'a black ocean' and 'the hope of the slave', 'Still I Rise' brings to life a Black woman's inspiring refusal to sink under the weight of racism. At the same time, the poem speaks to all humankind—to the capacity of every individual not just to rise up from whatever pain, sorrow, grief and heartache they have endured but to dance like they've got diamonds at the meeting of their thighs.

COURAGE
by ANNE SEXTON

It is in the small things we see it.
The child's first step,
as awesome as an earthquake.
The first time you rode a bike,
wallowing up the sidewalk.
The first spanking when your heart
went on a journey all alone.
When they called you crybaby
or poor or fatty or crazy
and made you into an alien,
you drank their acid
and concealed it.

Later,
if you faced the death of bombs and bullets
you did not do it with a banner,
you did it with only a hat to
cover your heart.
You did not fondle the weakness inside you
though it was there.
Your courage was a small coal
that you kept swallowing.
If your buddy saved you
and died himself in so doing,
then his courage was not courage,
it was love; love as simple as shaving soap.

Later,
if you have endured a great despair,
then you did it alone,

→

getting a transfusion from the fire,
picking the scabs off our heart,
then wringing it out like a sock.
Next, my kinsman, you powdered your sorrow,
you gave it a back rub
and then you covered it with a blanket
and after it had slept a while
it woke to the wings of the roses
and was transformed.

Later,
when you face old age and its natural conclusion
your courage will still be shown in the little ways,
each spring will be a sword you'll sharpen,
those you love will live in a fever of love,
and you'll bargain with the calendar
and at the last moment
when death opens the back door
you'll put on your carpet slippers
and stride out.

---

*In 'Courage', the Pulitzer Prize winning American poet Anne Sexton (1928–1974) reflects
on the bravery humans exhibit from our first step to our last. She is straightforward but
compassionate as she recounts life's hardships, gently reminding us that courage is always
with us, that sorrow can be transformed and that sometimes, when tenacity is not enough,
love can save us. Courage keeps us moving forward, right to life's 'natural conclusion'. In
the final poignant stanza, which describes an elderly person meeting death, readers are
comforted by an image of a brave soul who puts on carpet slippers and softly, but with
conviction, strides out.*

INVICTUS
by WILLIAM ERNEST HENLEY

Out of the night that covers me,
    Black as the pit from pole to pole,
I thank whatever gods may be
    For my unconquerable soul.

In the fell clutch of circumstance
    I have not winced nor cried aloud.
Under the bludgeonings of chance
    My head is bloody, but unbowed.

Beyond this place of wrath and tears
    Looms but the Horror of the shade,
And yet the menace of the years
    Finds and shall find me unafraid.

It matters not how strait the gate,
    How charged with punishments the scroll,
I am the master of my fate,
    I am the captain of my soul.

The images in 'Invictus' by the English poet William Ernest Henley (1849–1903) are terrifying. Night is 'black as the pit' and stretches 'from pole to pole'. The speaker's 'circumstance'—his condition of being—is in a 'fell clutch', that is, a fierce, sinister grasp. Moreover, he is not being merely beaten by chance, he's being bludgeoned. And yet, though the 'Horror of the shade' is looming, the speaker is in undaunted. The final, powerful line, 'I am the captain of my soul', demonstrates the speaker's self-awareness of his inner strength—his resilience. Though he is bloody, his head is 'unbowed'. He will not kneel before life's hardships.

LINES ON RETIREMENT, AFTER READING *LEAR*
by DAVID WRIGHT

for Richard Pacholski

Avoid storms. And retirement parties.
You can't trust the sweetnesses your friends will
offer, when they really want your office,
which they'll redecorate. Beware the still
untested pension plan. Keep your keys. Ask
for more troops than you think you'll need. Listen
more to fools and less to colleagues. Love your
youngest child the most, regardless. Back to
storms: dress warm, take a friend, don't eat the grass,
don't stand near tall trees, and keep the yelling
down—the winds won't listen, and no one will
see you in the dark. It's too hard to hear
you over all the thunder. But you're not
Lear, except that we can't stop you from what
you've planned to do. In the end, no one leaves
the stage in character—we never see
the feather, the mirror held to our lips.
So don't wait for skies to crack with sun. Feel
the storm's sweet sting invade you to the skin,
the strange, sore comforts of the wind. Embrace
your children's ragged praise and that of friends.
Go ahead, take it off, take it all off.
Run naked into tempests. Weave flowers
into your hair. Bellow at cataracts.
If you dare, scream at the gods. Babble as
if you thought words could save. Drink rain like cold
beer. So much better than making theories.
We'd all come with you, laughing, if we could.

In the American creative writing instructor and poet David Wright's 'Lines on Retirement, after Reading Lear', the good-natured speaker draws on the life of Shakespeare's King Lear, and especially his experience in the raging storm (act 3, scene 2), to offer advice on how to enjoy our golden years. Life is hard. Our children disappoint us—even our favourite ones. They stress us out till we think we'll go mad (some of us do). We want more than we are allowed to keep. We sulk and rage. We realise, possibly too late, that we have everything we need. This is Lear's experience and it might be yours. Make the best of it, this poem suggests. Seize the day. 'Don't wait for skies to crack with sun.'

COURAGE
by ELLA WHEELER WILCOX

There is a courage, a majestic thing
    That springs forth from the brow of pain, full-grown,
    Minerva-like, and dares all dangers known,
And all the threatening future yet may bring;
Crowned with the helmet of great suffering,
    Serene with that grand strength by martyrs shown,
    When at the stake they die and make no moan,
And even as the flames leap up are heard to sing.

A courage so sublime and unafraid,
    It wears its sorrows like a coat of mail;
And fate, the archer, passes by dismayed,
    Knowing his best barbed arrows needs must fail
To pierce a soul so armoured and arrayed
    That Death himself might look on it and quail.

Courage takes on a life of its own in this poem by the American poet and journalist Ella Wheeler Wilcox (1850–1919). She 'springs forth' as our greatest defender, battling her adversaries (and ours), whom she wears like a 'coat of mail'. Her experience with pain, suffering and fear leaves her with battle scars but, though she is bloody, her head is not bowed. (See Henley's 'Invictus' on p. 33, which gives us this marvellous image.) Courage is not only ferocious, she is also wise. Bearing such qualities, she is like Minerva, the Roman goddess of wisdom and war. Strong enough to subdue even fate and death, Courage is truly a 'majestic thing'.

DON'T QUIT
by JOHN GREENLEAF WHITTIER

When things go wrong as they sometimes will,
When the road you're trudging seems all up hill,
When the funds are low and the debts are high
And you want to smile, but you have to sigh,
When care is pressing you down a bit,
Rest if you must, but don't you quit.
Life is strange with its twists and turns
As every one of us sometimes learns
And many a failure comes about
When he might have won had he stuck it out;
Don't give up though the pace seems slow—
You may succeed with another blow.
Success is failure turned inside out—
The silver tint of the clouds of doubt,
And you never can tell just how close you are,
It may be near when it seems so far;
So stick to the fight when you're hardest hit—
It's when things seem worst that you must not quit.

John Greenleaf Whittier (1807-1892) was a driving force behind the abolishment of slavery in the United States. He is also remembered for his poetry. Despite the complexities of his political life, many of his poems are beautifully simple. Reading 'Don't Quit', with its fairly regular rhythm and consistent rhyming couplets, is in many ways like engaging in steady, rhythmic meditative breathing. Doing either brings a few moments of clarity and simplicity to our complex lives and encourages us to keep moving forward even in trying times.

Joy

No matter what joy is or where it comes from, one thing is certain:
it is one of the most positive emotions we experience.

What is joy? If you turn to a dictionary for a definition, you will find it is somewhat lacklustre. It doesn't spill off the page like joy itself. It doesn't wrap you in a warm hug and fill you with pleasure and satisfaction. Maybe this is why poets devote so much energy to trying to find words for the ineffable experience of being joyful.

For some people, joy is a deeply-rooted emotion. It derives from the knowledge that we are inherently valuable, that we are profoundly and meaningfully connected with one another and with other living things. For others, joy comes from the outside. It washes over us in the crisp, electric air of new love or shines on us when we achieve a goal we have set for ourselves. Some might call this *happiness*—a sister to joy. It's true that the two are sometimes indistinguishable from each other. If we had to make a distinction, we might say that happiness comes and goes, whereas joy, though it may falter, is ultimately steadfast.

No matter what joy is or where it comes from, one thing is certain: it is one of the most positive emotions we experience. It fills us with brightness and light. We actually *radiate* joy. If you are a joyful person, you have probably noticed how spontaneously others are drawn to you. They come into your sphere, catch your joy and spread it along. In this way, joy has the potential to improve humanity. How wonderfully powerful!

Joy is also a well of strength that we can draw from when life's heartaches, disappointments and frustrations threaten to drain our spirits. It is a protective covering too. When we choose to gird ourselves with the armour of joy, even powerful, unrelenting assailants find us difficult to defeat. And yet, for all its power, joy sometimes wavers in the overwhelm of sorrow. Gibran thinks about the relationship between the two in 'On Joy and Sorrow' (p. 45), recognising that both dwell in every human. In cases where sorrow eclipses your joy, what do you do to nurture the more welcome guest?

The poets in this section express different ways to cultivate this powerful emotion. Though they may predate the age of modern psychology, the poems each intuitively engage in the very practices mental health experts recommend. Levertov's speaker ('Of Being', p. 47) shifts the way she thinks about the ephemeral nature of happiness, fostering joy by focusing on the near-perfect present moment. The nanny in Blake's 'Nurse's Song' (p. 48) shows kindness to others. Wilde's speaker spends time in the great outdoors in 'Magdalen Walks' (p. 50). Though the poets in this section don't advocate it explicitly, reducing our time on social media is a practice almost every authority recommends. Just by reading this book, you are seeking joy by being away from your phone or computer.

If it's nice outside today, take this anthology outside, find a wide-open space in a park or on a beach, and, if possible, read some of these poems aloud. We think you will find that they define and inspire joy in ways a dictionary never could. They dance along the tongue with rhyme, rhythm and song and flood the heart and mind with joy.

HOW TO TRIUMPH LIKE A GIRL
by ADA LIMÓN

I like the lady horses best,
how they make it all look easy,
like running 40 miles per hour
is as fun as taking a nap, or grass.
I like their lady horse swagger,
after winning. Ears up, girls, ears up!
But mainly, let's be honest, I like
that they're ladies. As if this big
dangerous animal is also a part of me,
that somewhere inside the delicate
skin of my body, there pumps
an 8-pound female horse heart,
giant with power, heavy with blood.
Don't you want to believe it?
Don't you want to lift my shirt and see
the huge beating genius machine
that thinks, no, it knows,
it's going to come in first.

---

*In the joyful free verse poem 'How to Triumph Like a Girl', the American poet Ada Limón
(b. 1976) inspires confidence in every girl or woman who has ever felt overcome by the
world. The poem opens with a candid declaration in the first-person voice: 'I like the lady
horses best'. The speaker is intimate and enthusiastic as she considers our 'huge beating
genius machine', a heart that pumps life throughout our miraculous bodies. It's impossible
not to feel our own strength surge as we listen in. She then speaks to us directly, asking us
if we want to see her giant heart—and naturally, we do.*

ON JOY AND SORROW
by KAHLIL GIBRAN

Then a woman said, Speak to us of *Joy and Sorrow*.
And he answered:
Your joy is your sorrow unmasked.
And the selfsame well from which your laughter rises was
    oftentimes filled with your tears.
And how else can it be?
The deeper that sorrow carves into your being, the more joy
    you can contain.
Is not the cup that holds your wine the very cup that was burned
    in the potter's oven?

And is not the lute that soothes your spirit, the very wood that
was hollowed with knives?

When you are joyous, look deep into your heart and you shall
find it is only that which has given you sorrow that is giving
you joy.

When you are sorrowful look again in your heart, and you shall
see that in truth you are weeping for that which has been
your delight.

Some of you say, 'Joy is greater than sorrow,' and others say,
'Nay, sorrow is the greater.'

But I say unto you, they are inseparable.

Together they come, and when one sits alone with you at
your board, remember that the other is asleep upon your bed.

Verily you are suspended like scales between your sorrow
and your joy.

Only when you are empty are you at standstill and balanced.

When the treasure-keeper lifts you to weigh his gold and
his silver, needs must your joy or your sorrow rise or fall.

Kahlil Gibran (1883–1931) was among the best-selling American poets of the twentieth
century. He arrived in the United States from Lebanon in 1885 and established himself as
a painter and writer of both Arabic and English works. He is most commonly remembered
for his English book, The Prophet. In the straightforward study of joy and sorrow
presented in the poem here, the teacher proposes that joy can only be measured against
sorrow—that humans can't have one without the other. There is comfort in this: as
certainly as sorrow rises, so does it set and joy surges up in its place.

OF BEING
by DENISE LEVERTOV

I know this happiness
is provisional:

       the looming presences—
       great suffering, great fear—

       withdraw only
       into peripheral vision:

but ineluctable this shimmering
of wind in the blue leaves:

this flood of stillness
widening the lake of sky:

this need to dance,
this need to kneel:
          this mystery:

So much hinges on the tiny word 'but' in this honest and spellbinding poem by the British-born American poet and activist Denise Levertov (1923–1997). In the first six lines, the speaker recognises that those foes to happiness, 'great suffering, great fear', are always with us. At the seventh line, the poem pivots on that powerful conjunction 'but', and what is joyful becomes its focal point: wind shimmering in the leaves, the azure lake of sky, stillness, dancing and mystery.

NURSE'S SONG (SONGS OF INNOCENCE)
by WILLIAM BLAKE

When the voices of children are heard on the green,
And laughing is heard on the hill,
My heart is at rest within my breast,
And everything else is still.

'Then come home, my children, the sun is gone down,
And the dews of night arise;
Come, come, leave off play, and let us away
Till the morning appears in the skies.'

'No, no, let us play, for it is yet day,
And we cannot go to sleep;
Besides, in the sky the little birds fly,
And the hills are all cover'd with sheep.'

'Well, well, go and play till the light fades away,
And then go home to bed.'
The little ones leapèd and shoutèd and laugh'd
And all the hills echoèd.

---

*Both caregiver and nature are kindly and indulgent in 'Nurse's Song' by William
Blake (1757–1827), an English poet, illustrator and mystic whose fame has increased
immeasurably over the centuries. Few verses capture the pleasure of children at play in
the great outdoors like this sprightly poem, whose rhythm gallops along as the children
leap and shout 'on the green'. The poem's delightful final lines reflect the joyful relationship
between children and nature: the hills are alive with the echo of the children's laughter.*

AFTERNOON ON A HILL
by EDNA ST. VINCENT MILLAY

I will be the gladdest thing
    Under the sun!
I will touch a hundred flowers
    And not pick one.

I will look at cliffs and clouds
    With quiet eyes,
Watch the wind bow down the grass,
    And the grass rise.

And when lights begin to show
    Up from the town,
I will mark which must be mine,
    And then start down!

The American poet and playwright Edna St. Vincent Millay (1892–1950) had a prolific literary career. In 'Afternoon on a Hill', the speaker uses simple quatrains to express her delight in spending a day in the great outdoors. In many ways reflecting Wilde's spirited descriptions of nature in 'Magdalen Walks' (p. 50), Millay's poem paints a picture of flowers flourishing in the sun, grass rising in the wind and lights twinkling in the darkening sky. The vitality of nature mirrors the speaker's buoyant, determined spirit and readers inevitably capture her infectious joy.

MAGDALEN WALKS
by OSCAR WILDE

The little white clouds are racing over the sky,
  And the fields are strewn with the gold of the flower of March,
  The daffodil breaks under foot, and the tasselled larch
Sways and swings as the thrush goes hurrying by.

A delicate odour is borne on the wings of the morning breeze,
  The odour of leaves, and of grass, and of newly upturned earth,
  The birds are singing for joy of the Spring's glad birth,
Hopping from branch to branch on the rocking trees.

And all the woods are alive with the murmur and sound of Spring,
  And the rose-bud breaks into pink on the climbing briar,
  And the crocus-bed is a quivering moon of fire
Girdled round with the belt of an amethyst ring.

And the plane to the pine-tree is whispering some tale of love
  Till it rustles with laughter and tosses its mantle of green,
  And the gloom of the wych-elm's hollow is lit with the iris sheen
Of the burnished rainbow throat and the silver breast of a dove.

See! the lark starts up from his bed in the meadow there,
  Breaking the gossamer threads and the nets of dew,
  And flashing adown the river, a flame of blue!
The kingfisher flies like an arrow, and wounds the air.

THE BiRDS ARE SiNGING

Everything shimmers with life in the celebrated Irish poet and dramatist Oscar Wilde's
(1854–1900) 'Magdalen Walks'. Clouds are racing, birds are singing for joy and trees
are rustling in the glorious dawn of spring. The speaker's senses are awakened: he sees
fields strewn with flowers, smells new grass, and hears the woods waking up. The poem's
structure and rhyme scheme are formal and controlled, but the joyful images refuse to be
bridled, instead running wild and rampant over edges of lines onto new ones.

Nature
+
Escape

Even when she is at her most terrifying, nature is a place where
we can come to know ourselves and rewrite our own stories.

Nature is a kindly mother and a resilient one. Humankind has made astonishing advancements in science and technology, but many of these have had painful consequences for the Earth. Our clear-cutting has disrobed Mother Nature of her great green cloak. Our smog and soot have polluted her skies. Our modern systems of agriculture have drained her of life-giving waters. And yet, she endures and keeps offering of herself. In times of trouble, we seek restoration in her cool shade and we find solace in her grassy meadows. Her snow-capped mountains and crystalline lakes offer an escape from the very civilisation we have dedicated ourselves to building up.

Even when she is at her most terrifying, nature is a place where we can come to know ourselves and rewrite our own stories. King Lear, after being exposed to nature's wildest elements out on the heath, feels empathy for the first time and unfolds into a more humane version of himself. Of those less-fortunate than he, Lear says, 'Poor naked wretches, whereso'er you are / That bide the pelting of this pitiless storm, / How shall your houseless heads and unfed sides, / Your looped and windowed raggedness defend you / From seasons such as these? O I have ta'en / Too little care of this' (3.4.28–33). Even when she is not raging along with Lear, nature is an invigorating guide. Henry David Thoreau, the great nineteenth-century naturalist and philosopher, famously said, 'I went to the woods because I wished to live deliberately, to front only the essential facts of life, and see if I could not learn what it had to teach, and not, when I came to die, discover that I had not lived'.

Nature heals herself and heals us. She has patiently waited for us to remember that communing respectfully with her is crucial to the sustainability of the countless species to whom she offers herself as a dwelling place. This relationship is also vital to the longevity of nature herself. The natural historian Sir David Attenborough applauds the generations who are rising up to save their generous mother: 'Young people—they care. They know that this is the world that they're going to grow up in, that they're going to spend the rest of their lives in. But, I think it's more idealistic than that. They actually believe that humanity has no right to destroy and despoil regardless'.

The poets in this section celebrate nature's power, mystery, beauty and endurance. They find words for the joy she brings us and express gratitude for her goodness. Some poets extend their experience with nature to the sky. Wordsworth takes an aerial view in 'I Wandered Lonely as a Cloud' (p. 56) and then recalls the scenes upon returning home. Magee Jr. soars jubilantly through the 'long delirious, burning blue' in his aeroplane in 'High Flight' (p. 59). Other poets consider how we share space with nature or bring her into our own sphere. Stevenson captures the glee of speeding past not only meadows and rivers but also houses and hedges in 'From a Railway Carriage' (p. 63) while Bethell contemplates the allure of gardens in 'Time' (p. 64).

When we can't escape into nature physically, we can still retreat into her wide-open arms in the calming, healing green and blue spaces that the poets so lusciously describe.

I WANDERED LONELY AS A CLOUD
by WILLIAM WORDSWORTH

I wandered lonely as a cloud
That floats on high o'er vales and hills,
When all at once I saw a crowd,
A host, of golden daffodils;
Beside the lake, beneath the trees,
Fluttering and dancing in the breeze.

Continuous as the stars that shine
And twinkle on the milky way,
They stretched in never-ending line
Along the margin of a bay:
Ten thousand saw I at a glance,
Tossing their heads in sprightly dance.

The waves beside them danced; but they
Out-did the sparkling waves in glee:
A poet could not but be gay,
In such a jocund company:
I gazed—and gazed—but little thought
What wealth the show to me had brought:

For oft, when on my couch I lie
In vacant or in pensive mood,
They flash upon that inward eye
Which is the bliss of solitude;
And then my heart with pleasure fills,
And dances with the daffodils.

'I Wandered Lonely as a Cloud' by the English Romantic poet William Wordsworth (1770-1850) captures the profound union of humans and nature in a story of an aimless wanderer whose communion with the outdoors brings him pleasure long after he has left the 'jocund' (cheerful) company of daffodils. In the opening line the speaker equates himself with a floating cloud. From this vantage point, he can take in the full glory of the land and water below. As with 'Magdalen Walks' by Oscar Wilde (p. 50), the speaker's thoughts often spill over one line onto the next in a literary device known as enjambement. In Wordsworth's poem, this design gives dramatic force to the speaker's ecstatic meditation on his experience in nature: the fullness of his adventure cannot be contained by end-stopped lines.

SOMETHING TOLD THE WILD GEESE
by RACHEL FIELD

Something told the wild geese
It was time to go.
Though the fields lay golden
Something whispered,—'Snow.'
Leaves were green and stirring,
Berries, luster-glossed,
But beneath warm feathers
Something cautioned,—'Frost.'
All the sagging orchards
Steamed with amber spice,
But each wild breast stiffened
At remembered ice.
Something told the wild geese
It was time to fly,—
Summer sun was on their wings,
Winter in their cry.

There is a great mystery in nature that the American poet and novelist Rachel Field (1894–
1942) subtly captures in her richly-imaged 'Something Told the Wild Geese'. Nature's
enigmatic power is introduced in the first line with the open-ended word 'Something'. What
force alerts the wild geese that winter is looming when fields are golden, leaves are green
and trees are heavy with fruit? This ambiguous word appears four times, underscoring the
mystery of the changing seasons and allowing readers to wonder at nature's command. The
mystery is left unresolved. The geese, with sharper instincts than the human marveller, take
flight. The poet refuses to destroy the moment's magic by turning to science for answers,
preferring the way art allows humans to revel in nature's complexities.

HIGH FLIGHT
by JOHN GILLESPIE MAGEE JR.

Oh! I have slipped the surly bonds of earth
And danced the skies on laughter-silvered wings;
Sunward I've climbed, and joined the tumbling mirth
Of sun-split clouds—and done a hundred things
You have not dreamed of—wheeled and soared and swung
High in the sunlit silence. Hov'ring there
I've chased the shouting wind along, and flung
My eager craft through footless halls of air.

Up, up the long delirious, burning blue,
I've topped the windswept heights with easy grace
Where never lark, or even eagle flew—
And, while with silent lifting mind I've trod
The high unsurpassed sanctity of space,
Put out my hand and touched the face of God.

John Gillespie Magee Jr. (1922–1941), born in China to an American father and British mother, served with the Royal Canadian Air Force during World War II. Although his brief career as a fighter pilot (he died at 19) was fraught with harrowing sweeps over France and nerve-racking air defences in the English skies, 'High Flight' celebrates the liberty he experienced in an aeroplane. The poem opens with a joyous declaration: 'Oh! I have slipped the surly bonds of earth'. The alliterative s's in the first line continue throughout, with an effect that is at turns invigorating and soothing. Everywhere, though, there is the sacredness of freedom the pilot experiences in 'the high unsurpassed sanctity of space'.

ON THE DAY THE WORLD BEGINS AGAIN
by ARMAND GARNET RUFFO

On the day the world begins again
will it be the strongest animal
the swiftest bird
or the tiniest insect
that carries the news to humankind
announces rebirth in a roar
in a squeak or maybe in silence?

On the day the world begins again
will luminous light
rise from parting clouds
in unquestionable power
and refract a miraculous prism of colour
while the tallest white pine announces peace
in a sprinkling of communion?

On the day the world begins again
will those suspended behind bars
in and between grey ugliness
in their deadened shouts of protest
float beyond their circle of cigarette burns
and crude tattoos
beyond their sharp cries of where
they are and wish they were?

On the day the world begins again
will their re/imagined selves
the shape of thought
the shape of prayer
bend like molten steel
in the fire at the centre of the human heart
Will they rise beyond themselves
and find their way home
On the day the world begins again
will the cages open for them?

Armand Garnet Ruffo (b. 1955) is a member of the Chapleau Fox Lake Cree First Nation. His collaborative video-poem 'On the Day the World Begins Again' (vimeo. com/336947329) has incarcerated Indigenous Peoples at its heart. For many of the earliest human inhabitants of what later became called Canada, the land and waters are sacred and they live in relationship with nature. Today, disproportionately high numbers are incarcerated as a legacy of colonialism. Behind bars, they are cut off from the land. Nature, too, is suffering. Much work needs to be done to heal the rifts between people and nature, and between diverse people. But in every spirit, human and other-than-human, dwells 'unquestionable power'. And so, when 'luminous light' rises 'from parting clouds' and humans are reunited with the Earth, every spirit can find its way home.

AND THERE iS THE GREEN FOR STRINGING THE DAiSiES!

FROM A RAILWAY CARRIAGE
by ROBERT LOUIS STEVENSON

Faster than fairies, faster than witches,
Bridges and houses, hedges and ditches;
And charging along like troops in a battle,
All through the meadows the horses and cattle:
All of the sights of the hill and the plain
Fly as thick as driving rain;
And ever again, in the wink of an eye,
Painted stations whistle by.

Here is a child who clambers and scrambles,
All by himself and gathering brambles;
Here is a tramp who stands and gazes;
And there is the green for stringing the daisies!
Here is a cart run away in the road
Lumping along with man and load;
And here is a mill and there is a river:
Each a glimpse and gone for ever!

If there was ever an inspiration for basking in the present rather than worrying about the future or regretting the past, it is in 'From a Railway Carriage' by the Scottish writer, Robert Louis Stevenson (1850–1894). The poet captures the excitement of a child on a train that is winging its way past bridges, meadows and brightly painted stations. The destination is irrelevant; the journey is the focus of celebration in Stevenson's poem. We live vicariously through the thrilled young passenger as she takes in the sights around her. The train's speed is reflected in the poem's exhilarating rhythm. Everything is alive in this magical world of locomotion.

TIME
by URSULA BETHELL

'Established' is a good word, much used in garden books,
'The plant, when established'...
Oh, become established quickly, quickly, garden!
For I am fugitive, I am very fugitive—

Those that come after me will gather these roses,
And watch, as I do now, the white wistaria
Burst, in the sunshine, from its pale green sheath.

Planned. Planted. Established. Then neglected,
Till at last the loiterer by the gate will wonder
At the old, old cottage, the old wooden cottage,
And say 'One might build here, the view is glorious;
This must have been a pretty garden once.'

Humankind delights in cultivating the natural world. Though Mother Nature will always
reassert herself, our relationship with the land can be a peaceful one. This contemplation
comforts readers in 'Time', by the poet and social worker from New Zealand, (Mary) Ursula
Bethell (1874–1945). The landscape the humans 'establish'—a recurring word in the poem
that reflects our desire for curated spaces—takes on its own life after we have left it, but
traces of us remain. This is another theme in Bethell's free verse poem: the impermanence
of humankind. We will continue to leave our stamp, but our lives are fleeting compared with
the enduring epochs of nature.

Love

'Love' is a tiny word for a drive that bears, believes, hopes and endures all things.

'Love' is a tiny word for a drive that bears, believes, hopes and endures all things. The Ancient Greeks had multiple words to characterise humankind's most desired abstraction. *Eros*, or erotic love, is forceful and energetic. This electrically intense love fuels history's—and Hollywood's—greatest romances, from *Romeo and Juliet* to *Anna Karenina* to *Brokeback Mountain*. Lovers in love, as Donne's 'The Sun Rising' (p. 70) illuminates, know no world except their own. In this way, it is deeply selfish. But oh! what glorious self-centredness.

Dramatically different from *eros* is *agape*, or selfless love. This is the unconditional love that propels our compassion, our empathy and our goodness. It fuels heroic feats of sacrifice, such as rescuing strangers from trauma. It also inspires simpler acts of kindness, such as spending time with elderly people in a retirement home or volunteering at a food bank. Mother Teresa's lifework epitomises the 'love in action' that is *agape*.

Philia is affectionate love. It is Piglet's love for Pooh. Diana's for Anne of Green Gables. Alas, as Lysander quipped in *A Midsummer Night's Dream*, 'The course of true love never did run smooth' and sometimes *philia* and *eros* butt heads when one friend—and not the other—is hit with Cupid's arrow. Unlike *eros*, which is a sort of sexually charged sucker punch, *philia* is 'soft as the nesting dove', as Dunbar writes in 'Invitation to Love' (p. 72).

Another variety of love is *storge*, or instinctual love. This is the love that compels a famished mother to feed her daughter before herself. It is the love that fuels a father's night vigils as he cares for his suffering son. Some say the love of a parent for a child is the rawest, deepest love. Children, after all, fall from a star into our laps, as Duffy celebrates in 'The Light Gatherer' (p. 78).

Few people's guts twist into knots when they hear about *pragma*, or practical love, but this earthy, pragmatic love nourishes relationships in which *eros* may have mellowed but affection has not. *Pragma* is love that endures. It is the love that Golde has for Tevje in *Fiddler on the Roof.* The husband asks, 'Do you love me?' and the wife somewhat grudgingly replies, 'For twenty-five years I've lived with him, / Fought with him, starved with him / Twenty-five years my bed is his, / If that's not love, what is?'

There is also that delightfully playful, uncommitted love called *ludus*. Some might question the legitimacy of such an expression of love, but infatuated lovers across the ages swear zealously by it. This kind of love was immortalised in the American musical romantic comedy, *Grease*. A smitten Danny Zuko belts out, 'I got chills, / They're multiplyin' / And I'm losin' control. / 'Cause the power / You're supplyin', / It's electrifyin'!'

Finally comes *philautia*, or self-love. While such a love can lead to destructive self-absorption, *philautia* also shapes how we view ourselves in relation to the world. It is grounded in the ubiquitous belief that we can only love others if we first love ourselves. *Philautia* is the love that gently reminds us to practise self-care. It may be the form of love that compelled you to turn to the pages of this book, to search for rays of light shining through the dark.

THE SUN RISING
by JOHN DONNE

    Busy old fool, unruly sun,
      Why dost thou thus,
Through windows, and through curtains call on us?
Must to thy motions lovers' seasons run?
    Saucy pedantic wretch, go chide
    Late school boys and sour prentices,
  Go tell court huntsmen that the king will ride,
  Call country ants to harvest offices,
Love, all alike, no season knows nor clime,
Nor hours, days, months, which are the rags of time.

Thy beams, so reverend and strong
      Why shouldst thou think?
I could eclipse and cloud them with a wink,
But that I would not lose her sight so long;
      If her eyes have not blinded thine,
      Look, and tomorrow late, tell me,
   Whether both th' Indias of spice and mine
   Be where thou leftst them, or lie here with me.
Ask for those kings whom thou saw'st yesterday,
And thou shalt hear, All here in one bed lay.

      She's all states, and all princes, I,
      Nothing else is.
Princes do but play us; compared to this,
All honor's mimic, all wealth alchemy.
      Thou, sun, art half as happy as we,
      In that the world's contracted thus.
   Thine age asks ease, and since thy duties be
   To warm the world, that's done in warming us.
Shine here to us, and thou art everywhere;
This bed thy center is, these walls, thy sphere.

Very few poems capture the intensity and all-consuming nature of love like 'The Sun Rising'
by John Donne (1572–1631), an English poet as renowned for his often-racy love poems
as he is for his sacred ones. In this poem, lovers in love are a world unto themselves.
They know no season and recognise no time. The infatuated speaker audaciously proclaims
that nothing exists beyond the walls of the lovers' bedroom. The thrilling intensity of this
poem is in its direct address to the sun, who has dared to summon the lovers out of bed.
Refreshingly, they refuse. In a bold reordering of the cosmos, they command the sun to
shine exclusively on them. In doing so, the poem says, it warms the whole world.

INVITATION TO LOVE
by PAUL LAURENCE DUNBAR

Come when the nights are bright with stars
Or come when the moon is mellow;
Come when the sun his golden bars
Drops on the hay-field yellow.
Come in the twilight soft and gray,
Come in the night or come in the day,
Come, O love, whene'er you may,
And you are welcome, welcome.

You are sweet, O Love, dear Love,
You are soft as the nesting dove.
Come to my heart and bring it to rest
As the bird flies home to its welcome nest.

Come when my heart is full of grief
Or when my heart is merry;
Come with the falling of the leaf
Or with the redd'ning cherry.
Come when the year's first blossom blows,
Come when the summer gleams and glows,
Come with the winter's drifting snows,
And you are welcome, welcome.

*Paul Laurence Dunbar (1872–1906), one of the first Black poets in America to be
nationally acclaimed, speaks directly to Love in 'Invitation to Love'. The frequent repetition
of the imperative 'Come' highlights the speaker's urgent desire to possess this feeling. The
word is echoed in the more deferential phrase, 'welcome, welcome'. Love, after all, is a
mighty force. Still, the tone remains light and cheerful, with only one hint of sadness: an
invitation for Love to come when the heart is 'full of grief'. Every other image is pleasant;
even the snow is 'drifting', as though clearing the way for the triumphant entry of Love.*

FOR WOMEN WHO ARE 'DIFFICULT' TO LOVE
by WARSAN SHIRE

you are a horse running alone
and he tries to tame you
compares you to an impossible highway
to a burning house
says you are blinding him
that he could never leave you
forget you
want anything but you
you dizzy him, you are unbearable
every woman before or after you
is doused in your name
you fill his mouth
his teeth ache with memory of taste
his body just a long shadow seeking yours
but you are always too intense
frightening in the way you want him
unashamed and sacrificial
he tells you that no man can live up to the one who
lives in your head
and you tried to change didn't you?
closed your mouth more
tried to be softer
prettier
less volatile, less awake

but even when sleeping you could feel
him travelling away from you in his dreams
so what did you want to do, love
split his head open?
you can't make homes out of human beings
someone should have already told you that
and if he wants to leave
then let him leave
you are terrifying
and strange and beautiful
something not everyone knows how to love.

Warsan Shire (b. 1988) is a Somali-British poet and activist who was appointed the first Young Poet Laureate for London in 2014. In 'For Women Who Are "Difficult" to Love', Shire's speaker must come to terms with the truth that not all love lasts forever. But the poem does not end in disappointment. Ultimately, it celebrates the vigour of a 'strange and beautiful' woman — one whose heart is too fierce to be tamed and whose spirit is too wild to be broken. In this way, the poem recognises the importance of self-love and self-respect. As the insightful speaker observes, 'you can't make homes out of human beings'.

THE OASIS
by NAOMI REPLANSKY

I thought I held a fruit cupped in my hand.
Its sweetness burst
And loosed its juice. After long traveling,
After so long a thirst,
    I asked myself: Is this a drought-born dream?
    It was no dream.

I thought I slipped into a hidden room
Out of harsh light.
In cushioned dark, among rich furnishings,
There I restored my sight.
    Such luxury could never be for me!
    It was for me.

I thought I touched a mind that fitted mine
As bodies fit,
Angle to curve; and my mind throbbed to feel
The pulsing of that wit.
    This comes too late, I said. It can't be true!
    But it was true.

I thought the desert ended, and I felt
The fountains leap.
Then gratitude could answer gratitude
Till sleep entwined with sleep.
    Despair once cried: No passion's left inside!
    It lied. It lied.

The award-winning poet Naomi Replansky was born in New York in 1918, where she still resides over a century later. The daughter of Russian Jewish immigrants, Replansky showed an affinity for writing at an early age and as a young woman also became active in politics. There is nothing overtly political in her tender love poem, 'The Oasis', which expresses the feelings of wonder and gratitude a woman experiences when she realises the vibrancy and tenacity of love. The speaker candidly shares a poisonous thought experienced by humans since time immemorial—that love is not for her. The triumphant final line of each verse pronounces a marvellous counterclaim: her love is real, and she is worthy of it.

THE LIGHT GATHERER
by CAROL ANN DUFFY

When you were small, your cupped palms
each held a candlesworth under the skin,
enough light to begin,

        and as you grew,
light gathered in you, two clear raindrops
in your eyes,

        warm pearls, shy,
in the lobes of your ears, even always
the light of a smile after your tears.

Your kissed feet glowed in my one hand,
or I'd enter a room to see the corner you played in
lit like a stage set,

        the crown of your bowed head spotlit.
When language came, it glittered like a river,
silver, clever with fish,

        and you slept
with the whole moon held in your arms for a night light
where I knelt watching.

Light gatherer. You fell from a star
into my lap, the soft lamp at the bedside
mirrored in you,

and now you shine like a snowgirl,
a buttercup under a chin, the wide blue yonder
you squeal at and fly in,

like a jewelled cave,
turquoise and diamond and gold, opening out
at the end of a tunnel of years.

*Carol Ann Duffy (b. 1955) was the United Kingdom's first female poet laureate.
The Scottish poet is acclaimed for female-orientated love poems, many of them achingly
passionate or candidly erotic. 'The Light Gatherer' is also female-centred, but eros makes
way for the instinctual, unconditional love of a mother for her daughter. The devoted
parent tenderly observes her 'snowgirl', who brims with light as she passes through infancy
and youth. This luminescent child leaves brightness trailing behind her, as the glistening tails
of shooting stars.*

I HAVE SPREAD MY DREAMS UNDER YOUR FEET:

AEDH WISHES FOR THE CLOTHS OF HEAVEN
by WILLIAM BUTLER YEATS

Had I the heavens' embroidered cloths,
Enwrought with golden and silver light,
The blue and the dim and the dark cloths
Of night and light and the half light,
I would spread the cloths under your feet:
But I, being poor, have only my dreams;
I have spread my dreams under your feet;
Tread softly because you tread on my dreams.

The Irish writer William Butler Yeats (1865-1939) is among the most celebrated poets of the twentieth century. The image in 'Aedh Wishes for the Cloths of Heaven' of the richly embroidered fabric the lover would give his beloved if only he could is luxurious enough to win the coldest reader's heart. But nothing is so moving as the final picture of a lover giving the only thing he has: his dreams. The beloved has all the power as the enamoured speaker places his gift under her feet and begs her to 'tread softly'. The poignant variation on the fearful, hopeful lover giving his beloved his heart infuses the timeless image with new life, reminding readers that every experience of early love is harrowing and wonderful.

Tranquillity

'Wherever I go, there I am'. We cannot flee from ourselves
and therefore we must be at peace with ourselves.

Tranquillity is the convergence of a serene physical environment and a placid mind. This united inner and outer stillness may only be occasional in the turbulence of daily life, but by pursuing one we may also experience the other. We might feel the soft glow of tranquillity as we sit in a sunny window on a short break at work. We may savour it in the first hush after a blizzard, as we look out at the new snow from the warmth of an enclosed front porch. These moments of external quiet wend their way through us and fill us with an inner calm. They ready us for the tasks ahead.

The Roman philosopher and dramatist Seneca (c. 4 BCE–CE 65) was a keen observer of the inner life. He noted that feeling tranquil is impossible, no matter how peaceful the physical environment is, if the mind is unsettled: 'As Lucretius says:—"Thus every mortal from himself doth flee"; but what does he gain by so doing if he does not escape from himself?' (*De tranquillitate animi*, translation by Aubrey Stewart, 1900). This understanding that inner tranquillity is vital for a rich life is at the foundation of mindfulness, which is rooted in ancient forms of Hinduism and Buddhism but which has taken on more secular shapes as it has become popularised in the West. Seneca's insight dovetails perfectly with one that has been attributed to the Chinese philosopher, Confucius (c. 551–479 BCE): 'Wherever I go, there I am'. We cannot flee from ourselves and therefore we must be at peace with ourselves.

While a city can be quiet in the twilight hours or at the creeping in of the dawn, the peaceful surroundings most of the poets in this section describe are natural ones. A sweet, clear brook passing through an ancient wood. An unperturbed lake on whose surface shines the silver moon. Their soothing sounds and imagery can bring readers a sense of inner calm. When we enter these tranquil spaces either literally or in the world of the poems, we naturally lower our voices. Hushed, we 'swoon / Drunken with beauty' (Dutt, 'A Sea of foliage', p. 86). Studies have shown how these unrefined environments, far from the chaos of urban life, increase relaxation, reduce stress and alleviate pain in the humans who seek solace there.

Though these tranquil scenes are undisturbed by human noise, natural sounds may fill them with harmonious music. Bryant paints a verbal picture of cheerful rivulets sending forth glad sounds and trees alive with the music of birds in 'Inscription for the Entrance to a Wood' (p. 88). We seek to replicate these melodic sounds for children as we help them go to sleep. Tennyson brings the serenity of the outdoors into an infant's bedroom in his gentle lullaby, 'Sweet and Low' (p. 93). As adults, we also strive to soothe ourselves by creating our own peaceful environments when, as Wordsworth says, 'the world is too much with us'. This is exactly what Mansfield's speaker does in 'Camomile Tea' (p. 94). As the cacophony of the modern world jangles around us, we look for quiet spaces without as we seek serenity within.

SONNET: A SEA OF FOLIAGE GIRDS OUR GARDEN ROUND
by TORU DUTT

A sea of foliage girds our garden round,
    But not a sea of dull unvaried green,
    Sharp contrasts of all colors here are seen;
The light-green graceful tamarinds abound
Amid the mango clumps of green profound,
    And palms arise, like pillars gray, between;
    And o'er the quiet pools the seemuls lean,
Red-red, and startling like a trumpet's sound.
But nothing can be lovelier than the ranges
    Of bamboos to the eastward, when the moon
Looks through their gaps, and the white lotus changes
    Into a cup of silver. One might swoon
        Drunken with beauty then, or gaze and gaze
        On a primeval Eden, in amaze.

Toru Dutt (1856–1877) was a Bengali translator and writer who spent several years of her short life in Europe, sharpening her skills in English and French. In the poem here, Dutt cleverly blends the rhyme schemes of the Italian and Elizabethan sonnets in this carefully-crafted description of her family's garden at Baugmaree. The first quatrain brings us into a world of aquamarine and richly textured greens while the second quatrain draws on images that are more regal, with references to pillars and trumpets. The final quatrain and rhyming couplet, offset from the octave with the little word 'but', paint an image of her favourite part of the garden, 'ranges of bamboos'. Her illustration is so lush that we may 'swoon' with her as we gaze and gaze on her 'primeval Eden'.

INSCRIPTION FOR THE ENTRANCE TO A WOOD
by WILLIAM CULLEN BRYANT

Stranger, if thou hast learned a truth which needs
No school of long experience, that the world
Is full of guilt and misery, and hast seen
Enough of all its sorrows, crimes, and cares,
To tire thee of it, enter this wild wood
And view the haunts of Nature. The calm shade
Shall bring a kindred calm, and the sweet breeze
That makes the green leaves dance, shall waft a balm
To thy sick heart. Thou wilt find nothing here
Of all that pained thee in the haunts of men
And made thee loathe thy life. The primal curse
Fell, it is true, upon the unsinning earth,
But not in vengeance. God hath yoked to guilt
Her pale tormentor, misery. Hence, these shades
Are still the abodes of gladness: the thick roof
Of green and stirring branches is alive
And musical with birds, that sing and sport
In wantonness of spirit; while below
The squirrel, with raised paws and form erect,
Chirps merrily. Throngs of insects in the shade
Try their thin wings and dance in the warm beam
That waked them into life. Even the green trees
Partake the deep contentment; as they bend
To the soft winds, the sun from the blue sky

Looks in and sheds a blessing on the scene.
Scarce less the cleft-born wild-flower seems to enjoy
Existence, than the winged plunderer
That sucks its sweets. The massy rocks themselves,
And the old and ponderous trunks of prostrate trees
That lead from knoll to knoll a causey rude
Or bridge the sunken brook, and their dark roots,
With all their earth upon them, twisting high,
Breathe fixed tranquillity. The rivulet
Sends forth glad sounds, and tripping o'er its bed
Of pebbly sands, or leaping down the rocks,
Seems, with continuous laughter, to rejoice
In its own being. Softly tread the marge,
Lest from her midway perch thou scare the wren
That dips her bill in water. The cool wind,
That stirs the stream in play, shall come to thee,
Like one that loves thee nor will let thee pass
Ungreeted, and shall give its light embrace.

A long-time editor of the New-York Evening Post, *William Cullen Bryant (1794-1878)*
was also one of the most beloved American poets of his generation. 'Inscription for
the Entrance To a Wood' is an invitation to world-weary humans to seek peace in the
'haunts of Nature'. References to the 'sorrows, crimes, and cares' of the human world are
juxtaposed with soothing descriptions of the natural environment, where the 'sweet breeze'
is a 'balm / To thy sick heart'. So different from the inscription on the gate of Dante's
inferno, where travellers are told abandon hope, here in the peaceful arms of nature,
all wanderers may find peace.

THE LOST LAGOON
by E. PAULINE JOHNSON (TEKAHIONWAKE)

It is dusk on the Lost Lagoon,
And we two dreaming the dusk away,
Beneath the drift of a twilight grey,
Beneath the drowse of an ending day,
And the curve of a golden moon.

It is dark in the Lost Lagoon,
And gone are the depths of haunting blue,
The grouping gulls, and the old canoe,
The singing firs, and the dusk and—you,
And gone is the golden moon.

O! lure of the Lost Lagoon,—
I dream to-night that my paddle blurs
The purple shade where the seaweed stirs,
I hear the call of the singing firs
In the hush of the golden moon.

The poet-performer E. Pauline Johnson (1861–1913), also called Tekahionwake, was of Haudenosaunee (Iroquois) and British descent. The Lost Lagoon, which Tekahionwake named, is a small body of water near the entrance to the majestic Stanley Park in Vancouver, Canada. With its mesmerising images of dreamers on the lake at dusk, the poem is as tranquillising as the lagoon's quiet waters. When the skies grow too dark for the paddlers to see, other senses awaken, and the speaker hears firs singing to her 'in the hush of the golden moon'. Tekahionwake is buried very near the lagoon's peaceful shore.

A HYMN TO THE MOON
by LADY MARY WORTLEY MONTAGU

Written in July, in an arbour

Thou silver deity of secret night,
Direct my footsteps through the woodland shade;
Thou conscious witness of unknown delight,
The Lover's guardian, and the Muse's aid!
By thy pale beams I solitary rove,
To thee my tender grief confide;
Serenely sweet you gild the silent grove,
My friend, my goddess, and my guide.
E'en thee, fair queen, from thy amazing height,
The charms of young Endymion drew;
Veil'd with the mantle of concealing night;
With all thy greatness and thy coldness too.

A spirited woman who is remembered for her introduction of the smallpox inoculation into England, Lady Mary Wortley Montagu (1689–1762) was also a lifelong poet who pays homage to the 'silver deity of secret night' in 'A Hymn to the Moon'. In this guardian she confides her griefs and shares her trysts. The speaker is bound to the pale gilder of the 'silent grove' as a sister who is also in love – for the moon was enamoured of Endymion, that beautiful youth of Greek mythology. Together, they will seek out amorous pleasures in the quiet of the 'woodland shade'.

SWEET AND LOW (FROM *THE PRINCESS*)
by ALFRED, LORD TENNYSON

Sweet and low, sweet and low,
        Wind of the western sea,
Low, low, breathe and blow,
        Wind of the western sea!
Over the rolling waters go,
Come from the dying moon, and blow,
        Blow him again to me;
While my little one, while my pretty one, sleeps.

Sleep and rest, sleep and rest,
        Father will come to thee soon;
Rest, rest, on mother's breast,
        Father will come to thee soon;
Father will come to his babe in the nest,
Silver sails all out of the west
        Under the silver moon:
Sleep, my little one, sleep, my pretty one, sleep.

Alfred, Lord Tennyson (1809–1892) was one of the Victorian period's leading writers and successor to Wordsworth as England's poet laureate. The Princess is a long narrative poem interspersed with moving lyric pieces, such as 'Sweet and Low' which was put to music by the English composer, Sir Joseph Barnby (1838–1896). Since time immemorial, children have awaited the return of their fathers — or mothers — from sea. In this gentle lullaby, the poet appeals to the western wind to softly 'breathe and blow', to bring the traveller home. The alliteration running throughout the lyric is soothing, lulling the long-suffering child to sleep.

CAMOMILE TEA
by KATHERINE MANSFIELD

Outside the sky is light with stars;
There's a hollow roaring from the sea.
And, alas! for the little almond flowers,
The wind is shaking the almond tree.

How little I thought, a year ago,
In the horrible cottage upon the Lee
That he and I should be sitting so
And sipping a cup of camomile tea.

Light as feathers the witches fly,
The horn of the moon is plain to see;
By a firefly under a jonquil flower
A goblin toasts a bumble-bee.

We might be fifty, we might be five,
So snug, so compact, so wise are we!
Under the kitchen-table leg
My knee is pressing against his knee.

Our shutters are shut, the fire is low,
The tap is dripping peacefully;
The saucepan shadows on the wall
Are black and round and plain to see.

The speaker in the New Zealand poet and short fiction writer Katherine Mansfield's (1888–1923) 'Camomile Tea' never discloses what happened to her 'in the horrible cottage upon the Lee'. All we know is that difficulties in times past have faded into memory. Even the 'tap is dripping peacefully' in this soothing poem. There is magic outside—witches fly in a starlit sky and goblins carouse under the moon—but the real magic is inside, where two people in love sit together near the fire, sipping a cup of camomile tea.

Gratitude

While gratification is extrinsic, gratitude is more often intrinsic. It is a feeling of deep, sincere appreciation that we foster in spite of everything.

As children, we were happy with so little. We entered into the idyll of our imaginative worlds and found more than enough to make us grateful. The forest was our kingdom. Her mighty firs were our great castles and her melodious brooks were waterways to the dewy meadows we claimed as our own. We lazed in soft beds of green clover, wove golden buttercups into crowns, bathed in resplendent sunshine and wore the night sky's twinkling stars for jewels. In those magical days of play and rest, when we had not yet encountered the perplexities of adult life and when every need was met, it was easy to feel gratitude.

As adults, we began to seek material gratification to compensate for the responsibilities to which we were now subject. Everyday worries obscured our vision and compromised our capacity to be grateful. The nouns 'gratification' and 'gratitude' sound similar but they are vastly different. To be gratified is to have one's appetites or desires satisfied. Derived from the Latin verb for 'to bestow grace upon', it always comes from without. But humans are as the mythological Tantalus who is punished by perpetual dissatisfaction. Unfulfilled by what we have received and tortured by what we think we lack, we always seek more.

While gratification is extrinsic, gratitude is more often intrinsic. It is a feeling of deep, sincere appreciation that we foster in spite of everything. While we may feel gratitude for an external satisfaction, such as a job promotion or a cool breeze on an otherwise stifling day, at its heart, gratitude is a way of viewing the world that brings contentment regardless of the place in which we find ourselves. In saying thanks for everything, we cross over the chasm that separates gratification from gratitude.

While some studies have found that a lack of gratitude can be genetic, there is also evidence to suggest that practising gratitude can help even the most ungrateful people become more thankful and consequently happier. One way to stimulate gratefulness is to begin noticing those things we may be taking for granted, such as food, shelter or love. In Shakespeare's Sonnet 29 (p. 103), the speaker's life is in shambles, but his state of mind changes when he meditates on his beloved. The love that makes one grateful does not have to be romantic. It can be affectionate, playful, charitable and so on. The speaker in Issa's haiku (p. 105) is physically cold and yet his heart grows warm as thinks about the love he feels for the children in his life.

Neither Shakespeare nor Issa would have heard of the modern practice of keeping a gratitude journal, but they instinctively wrote out words of thankfulness. Another modern practice for cultivating gratefulness is simply to say 'thanks' aloud to the person to whom we feel grateful, even if we are alone. Sending them a note of thanks could boost your spirit and theirs.

These practices can strengthen the 'gratitude muscle' that may have atrophied as we became preoccupied with responsibility and stress. When these burdens threaten to overcome us, say the experts, practise gratitude anyway. The poets say the same: 'thank you we are saying and waving / dark though it is' (W.S. Merwin, 'Thanks', p. 106).

SONNET 39: BECAUSE THOU HAST THE POWER AND OWN'ST THE GRACE
by ELIZABETH BARRETT BROWNING

Because thou hast the power and own'st the grace
To look through and behind this mask of me
(Against which, years have beat thus blanchingly,
With their rains), and behold my soul's true face,
The dim and weary witness of life's race,—
Because thou hast the faith and love to see,
Through that same soul's distracting lethargy,
The patient angel waiting for his place
In the new Heavens,—because nor sin nor woe,
Nor God's infliction, nor death's neighbourhood,
Nor all which others viewing, turn to go,
Nor all which makes me tired of all, self-viewed,—
Nothing repels thee,—Dearest, teach me so
To pour out gratitude, as thou dost, good!

The Victorian poet Elizabeth Barrett Browning (1806–1861) was as respected among her peers as she is today. Her most beloved work is Sonnets from the Portuguese, from which this sonnet is taken. The speaker openly expresses her appreciation for a man who loves her unconditionally. Though from her perspective she is beleaguered in body and spirit, he pours his gratitude on her. He does this, she says, as freely as he pours out good, or goodness, from his own loving and faithful spirit. Yet, the poem is as clever as it is passionate, for it reveals that the speaker naturally possesses the thankful heart she so fervently desires.

FOR THY SWEET LOVE REMEMBERED

SONNET 29: WHEN IN DISGRACE
WITH FORTUNE AND MEN'S EYES
by WILLIAM SHAKESPEARE

When in disgrace with Fortune and men's eyes,
I all alone beweep my outcast state,
And trouble deaf heaven with my bootless cries,
And look upon myself and curse my fate,
Wishing me like to one more rich in hope,
Featured like him, like him with friends possessed,
Desiring this man's art, and that man's scope,
With what I most enjoy contented least;
Yet in these thoughts myself almost despising,
Haply I think on thee, and then my state,
Like to the lark at break of day arising
From sullen earth sings hymns at heaven's gate,
    For thy sweet love remembered such wealth brings
    That then I scorn to change my state with kings.

William Shakespeare (1564–1616), England's most distinguished writer, was a keen observer of the human spirit. In Sonnet 29, he describes the self-alienation, self-pity and self-loathing that feed that great devil, depression. The speaker weeps alone, prays to an absent god, derives no pleasure from his hobbies and falls into the deadly trap of comparing himself with others. How does he drive out the demon? He shifts his focus. Instead of dwelling on the lies depression mocks him with, he turns his thoughts to love and feels a rush of gratitude and joy.

THE LAST DAYS OF SUMMER BEFORE THE FIRST FROST
by TIM BOWLING

Here at the wolf's throat, at the egress of the howl,
all along the avenue of deer-blink and salmon-kick
where the spider lets its microphone down
into the cave of the blackberry bush—earth echo,
absence of the human voice—wait here
with a bee on your wrist and a fly on your cheek,
the tiny sun and tiny eclipse.
It is time to be grateful for the breath
of what you could crush without thought,
a moth, a child's love, your own life.
There might never be another chance.
How did you find me, the astonished mother says
to her four-year-old boy who'd disappeared
in the crowds at the music festival.
I followed my heart, he shrugs,
so matter-of-fact you might not see
behind his words
(o hover and feed, but not too long)

the bee trails turning to ice as they're flown.

Tim Bowling (b. 1964) is an award-winning Canadian novelist and poet. 'The Last Days of Summer', set on the cusp of the autumnal equinox, briefly relates a mother's experience of finding her child, who had become lost at a music festival. This fleeting narrative is the backdrop for a contemplation on ephemerality. The poem opens with an arresting image of a wolf on the verge of releasing a mighty howl. The animal's power is matched by our own: 'It is time to be grateful for the breath / of what you could crush without thought'. This surprise revelation that what we cherish is as delicate as summer flowers are to frost inspires us to hold tightly to those we love.

HAIKU
by ISSA

A heart full of thankfulness for the children, this cold night.

The Japanese poet Kobayashi Nobuyuki (1763–1828), known as Issa ('cup of tea'), is a master of the Japanese verse form, haiku. In English, haiku usually have three unrhymed lines with five, seven and five syllables, respectively. In Japanese, haiku are often arranged in a single vertical line of seventeen 'morae' (rhythmic units of speech something like syllables). This form is reflected (horizontally) in Issa's haiku in this collection. Notice there is not a verb in sight. Haiku masters prefer to dwell on sense and feeling, not action. The haiku's power is in its simple beauty, its incredible economy of space. In the short poem here, the speaker is grateful for the joy of children during a 'cold night'. The swiftness of the poem matches the rush of joy that practising gratitude can bring even during difficult times.

THANKS
by W.S. MERWIN

Listen
with the night falling we are saying thank you
we are stopping on the bridges to bow from the railings
we are running out of the glass rooms
with our mouths full of food to look at the sky
and say thank you
we are standing by the water thanking it
standing by the windows looking out
in our directions

back from a series of hospitals back from a mugging
after funerals we are saying thank you
after the news of the dead
whether or not we knew them we are saying thank you

over telephones we are saying thank you
in doorways and in the backs of cars and in elevators
remembering wars and the police at the door
and the beatings on stairs we are saying thank you
in the banks we are saying thank you
in the faces of the officials and the rich
and of all who will never change
we go on saying thank you thank you

with the animals dying around us
taking our feelings we are saying thank you
with the forests falling faster than the minutes
of our lives we are saying thank you
with the words going out like cells of a brain
with the cities growing over us
we are saying thank you faster and faster
with nobody listening we are saying thank you
thank you we are saying and waving
dark though it is

Almost everything that happens in the prolific American poet W.S. Merwin's 'Thanks' (1927–2019) is challenging. In between lightning-quick flashes of goodness—nourishing food, welcoming skies, refreshing waters—come tempests of inexorable hardships. Loss and grief. Climate change. Tyrannical corporate machines. But each strenuous moment is met, surprisingly, with thanks. Also intriguing is that the gratitude is expressed in the present tense. We are stopping. We are standing. We are saying thank you. To be mindful is to be aware of what is good in this moment—however intangible or provisional—and to take time to be grateful.

REFLECTIONS ON A GIFT OF WATERMELON PICKLE
RECEIVED FROM A FRIEND CALLED FELICITY
by JOHN TOBIAS

During that summer
When unicorns were still possible;
When the purpose of knees
Was to be skinned;
When shiny horse chestnuts
    (Hollowed out
    Fitted with straws
    Crammed with tobacco
    Stolen from butts
    In family ashtrays)
Were puffed in green lizard silence
While straddling thick branches
Far above and away
From the softening effects
Of civilization;

During that summer—
Which may never have been at all;
But which has become more real
Than the one that was—
Watermelons ruled.

Thick pink imperial slices
Melting frigidly on sun-parched tongues
Dribbling from chins;
Leaving the best part,
The black bullet seeds,
To be spit out in rapid fire
Against the wall

Against the wind
Against each other;

And when the ammunition was spent,
There was always another bite:
It was a summer of limitless bites,
Of hungers quickly felt
And quickly forgotten
With the next careless gorging.

The bites are fewer now.
Each one is savored lingeringly,
Swallowed reluctantly.

But in a jar put up by Felicity,
The summer which maybe never was
Has been captured and preserved.
And when we unscrew the lid
And slice off a piece
And let it linger on our tongue:
Unicorns become possible again.

If time travel is possible, this mid-twentieth-century poem by the American writer John Tobias is the portal. It offers readers a delicious study of nostalgia — indeed, one so flavourful that if a poem could be literally consumed, this would surely be the one to relish. Never has childhood seemed so divine. Being fettered by the past is miserable but finding joy in memories of simpler, freer times — however altered they have become in our mind's eye — is wondrous. And sometimes all we need is one scent, sound or taste for a pleasurable moment from bygone days to wash over us as sweet, soft rain.

Comfort

Poems can also bring comfort. Their form, rhythm,
sound, imagery and sense reassure us.

Life has many sorrows. Nietzsche said that to live is to suffer. But though there is a time for weeping and mourning, there is also a time for laughing and dancing, as the ancient book of Wisdom, *Ecclesiastes*, reassures us. The encouraging reminder that 'there is a time for everything' has echoed down the millennia, reappearing in this volume in Gay's 'Sorrow Is Not My Name' (p. 114).

It is natural in our darkest days to seek certain basic comforts. We may prepare warm food, take a long shower or bath or curl up with a good book. These are acts of self-care. Though summoning up the energy to reach out to others can be a monumental challenge, human touch can also be healing. A hug releases tension in the body, allowing us to rest and mend.

Humans are not alone in needing comfort. Elephants, dolphins, apes and some birds caress each other or make soothing sounds when they see one of their own experiencing stress. Humans are also driven to alleviate the suffering of others. We soothe our loved ones, beloved pets and sometimes even strangers with gentle touch or sweet, soft sounds. We also seek comfort from other animals. Think of how heartening it can be to stroke the soft fur of your cat or dog. Research shows that having a pet may reduce our stress and improve our physical health by decreasing our cortisol levels and lowering our blood pressure.

Poems can also bring comfort. Their form, rhythm, sound, imagery and sense reassure us. A poem may cascade briskly down a page or it may wind indolently in luxurious phrases that run over several lines. In either case, poems are distinct for the white space they leave on the page—those areas around and within the poem that cause readers to take a revitalising breath. The white space asks us to be silent for a few moments. It slows us down.

A poem's rhythm can also put us at greater ease. Not all poems have a rhythm, but those that do establish a regular pattern that can be reassuring. Consider the gentle, familiar iambic pentameter of a sonnet, which replicates the beats of a heart: *da-DUH, da-DUH, da-DUH, da-DUH, da-DUH*. 'Shall *I* com*pare* thee *to* a *sum*mer's *day*?' Not all poems rhyme either, but those with a consistent rhyme scheme can be grounding. Poems that repeat certain words or sounds also have a meditative effect. The hushed alliterative *f*s and *w*'s in Teasdale's 'A December Day' (p. 116) soothe the reader and the speaker as they encounter winter's 'feathery filigree of frost'.

The stories, states of mind or points of view that a poem makes vivid through language can reassure us too. In 'Up-Hill' (p. 119), Rossetti depicts life's pains as a long journey but reminds us that relief will come. When a poem gives words to the sorrows we endure, we may feel less alone.

Reading a poem out loud highlights its steady rhythms, reassuring rhymes, soothing alliterations and resonant images, thus making it especially comforting. Reading it more than once helps it to grow familiar, a beloved blanket we reach for in the cold. We may even commit a poem to memory and use it as a form of meditation. As we fall into its familiar cadences, we begin to feel a little more like ourselves.

SORROW IS NOT MY NAME
by ROSS GAY

—after Gwendolyn Brooks

No matter the pull toward brink. No
matter the florid, deep sleep awaits.
There is a time for everything. Look,
just this morning a vulture
nodded his red, grizzled head at me,
and I looked at him, admiring
the sickle of his beak.
Then the wind kicked up, and,
after arranging that good suit of feathers
he up and took off.
Just like that. And to boot,
there are, on this planet alone, something like two
million naturally occurring sweet things,
some with names so generous as to kick
the steel from my knees: agave, persimmon,
stick ball, the purple okra I bought for two bucks
at the market. Think of that. The long night,
the skeleton in the mirror, the man behind me
on the bus taking notes, yeah, yeah.
But look; my niece is running through a field
calling my name. My neighbor sings like an angel
and at the end of my block is a basketball court.
I remember. My color's green. I'm spring.

—for Walter Aikens

'Sorrow Is Not My Name' by the award-winning American poet and editor Ross Gay
(b. 1974) is a celebration of simple things in the face of life's uncertainty. Death is
everywhere in this poem: the brink; a vulture with a grizzled head and sickle for a beak;
a long night; a skeleton in a mirror. But death is not coming for the speaker today. He
is green. He is spring. He is taking delight in the 'two / million naturally occurring sweet
things' the Earth has to offer. The repeated 'No matter ... No / matter' in the opening lines
is a mantra, comforting readers in the same way the 'Shhhh.....shhhhh' that we heard as
children lulled us into sweet slumber.

A DECEMBER DAY
by SARA TEASDALE

Dawn turned on her purple pillow,
    And late, late, came the winter day;
Snow was curved to the boughs of the willow,
    The sunless world was white and grey.

At noon we heard a blue-jay scolding,
    At five the last cold light was lost
From blackened windows faintly holding
    The feathery filigree of frost.

In 'A December Day', by the American lyric poet Sara Teasdale (1884–1933), the speaker
finds comfort in the middle of a dark winter. The opening lines are so lovely that the final
line of the first quatrain is startling. We must go back to see that the imagery is starker
than we first thought. Dawn is not a glorious princess, basking in her own warm energy.
She is sluggish and her languid movements produce a 'sunless world'. When she finally
rises, it's not for long. Yet, the poem's final line reminds us that beauty exists even in the
dark and endures whether we can see it or not. Suspended in a snow-banked window is
a 'feathery filigree of frost'—a delicate pattern of ice. The alliteration is soft and gentle.
Winter has lost its sting.

THE DREAM KEEPER
by LANGSTON HUGHES

Bring me all of your dreams,
You dreamers,
Bring me all of your
Heart melodies
That I may wrap them
In a blue cloud-cloth
Away from the too-rough fingers
Of the world.

Langston Hughes (1902–1967) was a writer and activist from Missouri. As a young man he moved to New York, where he was an active figure in the Harlem Renaissance (1920s–1930s), a period when Harlem, in New York City, became a locus of creativity and intellectualism that began to shatter stereotypes of Black people in America. Hughes and his comrades, including Claude McKay (p. 17), were no strangers to the world's bigotry and injustice. In the poem here, the speaker encourages readers to never give up. He comforts them with the gentle image of a kindly dream keeper who will provide sanctuary for our dreams.

UP-HILL
by CHRISTINA ROSSETTI

Does the road wind up-hill all the way?
    Yes, to the very end.
Will the day's journey take the whole long day?
    From morn to night, my friend.

But is there for the night a resting-place?
    A roof for when the slow dark hours begin.
May not the darkness hide it from my face?
    You cannot miss that inn.

Shall I meet other wayfarers at night?
    Those who have gone before.
Then must I knock, or call when just in sight?
    They will not keep you standing at that door.

Shall I find comfort, travel-sore and weak?
    Of labour you shall find the sum.
Will there be beds for me and all who seek?
    Yea, beds for all who come.

Christina Rossetti (1830–1894) was one of the greatest poets of the Victorian era. The rhyming quatrains she uses in 'Up-Hill' are deceptively simple given the poem tackles the weighty theme of life's hard labours. The poem uses the metaphor of life as a journey and is written as a dialogue, with queries posed by a weary traveller and answers given by an honest, compassionate and omniscient stranger. Rossetti does not shrink from the fact that life has seasons of suffering – the road is up-hill 'to the very end'. But only the first quatrain lingers on that hard truth. With each successive question, the responder soothes the traveller with the assurance that rest awaits her.

LATE FRAGMENT
by RAYMOND CARVER

And did you get what
you wanted from this life, even so?
I did.
And what did you want?
To call myself beloved, to feel myself
beloved on the earth.

'Late Fragment' is the final poem in the last book by beloved American poet and writer
of short fiction, Raymond Carver (1938–1988). In this poignant verse, brief as life itself,
Carver reassures readers that material possessions are irrelevant at the end of our days.
The only thing we need is love.

IN BLACKWATER WOODS
by MARY OLIVER

Look, the trees
are turning
their own bodies
into pillars

of light,
are giving off the rich
fragrance of cinnamon
and fulfillment,

the long tapers
of cattails
are bursting and floating away over
the blue shoulders

of the ponds,
and every pond,
no matter what its
name is, is

nameless now.
Every year
everything
I have ever learned

in my lifetime
leads back to this: the fires
and the black river of loss
whose other side

is salvation,
whose meaning
none of us will ever know.
To live in this world

you must be able
to do three things:
to love what is mortal;
to hold it

against your bones knowing
your own life depends on it;
and, when the time comes to let it
go,
to let it go.

The award-winning American poet Mary Oliver's (1935–2019) 'In Blackwater Woods'
vividly describes a forest's luminous transformation. It invites us into its world with the
simple invitation, 'Look', as it offers a contemplation on surrender. We have all endured
losses. We have watched our lives as we knew them burn in the fire. When we are finally
able to relinquish the worst of the suffering, we experience a journey from grief to
deliverance, from wood to pillars of light. To try to understand loss is to drive ourselves
to the brink of madness. To accept it is salvation – but to achieve this we must be kind to
ourselves as we practise the bittersweet art of letting go.

Index

First published in 2021 by Frances Lincoln
an imprint of The Quarto Group.
The Old Brewery, 6 Blundell Street,
London, N7 9BH, United Kingdom
www.QuartoKnows.com